Unveiling the Invisible

Exploring Homelessness in Massachusetts

By

Dr. David K. Ewen, Minister

ISBN: 9798394575907

Cover Art: Ev on February 23, 2018
(Lyon, France) https://unsplash.com/@evstyle

Cover Art: Ev on February 23, 2018
(Lyon, France) https://unsplash.com/@evstyle

About the Book

"Unveiling the Invisible: Exploring Homelessness in Massachusetts" delves deep into the complex issue of homelessness in the state of Massachusetts. Authored by Dr. David K. Ewen, Minister, this thought-provoking book examines the historical context, current state, and various aspects surrounding homelessness in Massachusetts. Through a comprehensive analysis, the book sheds light on urban centers and homelessness hotspots, factors contributing to homelessness, and the unique challenges faced by special populations and homeless families. It also explores the initiatives, programs, and innovative approaches that have been implemented to address homelessness, as well as the role of advocacy and policy changes in effecting long-term solutions. With an eye towards the future, this book presents potential solutions and emphasizes the crucial role of society in fostering housing stability for all. "Unveiling the Invisible" offers valuable insights and inspires readers to engage with the issue of homelessness and work towards a more compassionate and inclusive society.

<u>About the Author</u>

Dr. David K. Ewen is a dedicated minister with a passion for serving the homeless community. With a profound commitment to making a difference in the lives of those in need, he devotes his time and expertise to weekly street ministry, where he provides support, nourishment, and spiritual guidance to individuals experiencing homelessness. Driven by compassion and a deep understanding of the challenges faced by the homeless, Dr. Ewen brings a unique perspective to the exploration of homelessness in his book. His firsthand experiences and unwavering dedication lend authenticity and empathy to his writing, inspiring readers to take action and engage with the issue on a personal and societal level. With his profound insights and commitment to social justice, Dr. David K. Ewen brings a powerful voice to the discussion surrounding homelessness in *"Unveiling the Invisible: Exploring Homelessness in Massachusetts."*

Dr. David K. Ewen, Minister

<u>Appreciation</u>

The dedication and involvement of individuals like Pastor Larry Freeman, Pastor Chris Pyrek, Pastor Robert Perreault, and Pastor Jack DesRoches (Founder: My Father's House), alongside other committed volunteers such as Pastors Jose Martinez, Pastor Melly Martinez, and Dr. David K. Ewen, Minister, speak volumes about their compassion and commitment to serving the homeless community.

The presence of these pastors and volunteers in Between Bridges Ministry demonstrates the power of collective action and highlights the importance of faith-based organizations in addressing the needs of marginalized populations. Their involvement shows that the ministry is not solely focused on providing physical necessities but also recognizes the significance of spiritual support in the lives of those experiencing homelessness.

The dedicated service of these pastors and volunteers extends beyond material assistance. Their active involvement in providing prayer during the weekly services at Between Bridges demonstrates a holistic approach to helping the homeless community. By addressing both the physical and spiritual needs of individuals, they offer a sense of hope, encouragement, and a reminder that they are valued and loved.

The involvement of a diverse group of pastors and volunteers within the ministry also brings a range of skills, perspectives, and experiences to the table. This collective expertise allows for a more comprehensive and inclusive approach to serving the homeless community, ensuring that different needs are met and that individuals from various backgrounds feel welcome and supported.

The efforts of Pastor Larry Freeman, Pastor Chris Pyrek, Pastor Robert Perreault, Pastor Jack DesRoches, and the dedicated team of pastors and volunteers at Between Bridges Ministry and My Father's House (founded by Pastor Jack DesRoches) serve as an inspiration and a reminder of the positive impact that individuals and faith-based organizations can have on their communities. Their commitment to serving the homeless population in Springfield, MA, not only provides essential support but also spreads compassion, understanding, and a message of hope to those who need it the most.

Dedication

To Pastor Larry Freeman, Pastor Chris Pyrek, Pastor Robert Perreault, and Pastor Jack DesRoches,

This book is dedicated to your unwavering commitment, compassion, and service to the homeless community in Springfield, MA. Your selfless dedication and tireless efforts have touched the lives of countless individuals and have made a profound impact on the community.

Through your leadership and involvement in Between Bridges Ministry, you have exemplified the true essence of Christian outreach. Your genuine care, empathy, and willingness to serve have provided hope, healing, and support to those who have found themselves in the depths of homelessness.

Your collective efforts, alongside the dedication of other pastors and volunteers, have created a haven where the homeless community is embraced, nourished, and uplifted. The impact of your work extends far beyond providing physical necessities; it extends to nourishing the souls and spirits of those you serve.

In this book, we seek to shine a light on the remarkable contributions you have made and continue to make in addressing homelessness. Your dedication has not gone unnoticed, and your unwavering faith and compassion have inspired others to join in the noble cause of serving those in need.

May this dedication serve as a testament to your profound impact and as a reminder of the transformative power of compassion and service. Thank you for your extraordinary commitment, and may your work continue to bring comfort, hope, and healing to the lives of the homeless community.

With deep gratitude,

Dr. David K. Ewen, Minister

May 2023

Table of Contents

[1] Introduction

Homelessness in Massachusetts has long been a pressing issue, with a history deeply rooted in economic fluctuations, social inequalities, and systemic challenges. From the Great Depression to the deinstitutionalization of mental health facilities in the 1970s, the state has witnessed waves of homelessness affecting individuals and families from various backgrounds. Today, Massachusetts continues to grapple with a significant homelessness problem, with over 20,000 individuals experiencing homelessness on any given night, including families, veterans, individuals with mental health issues, and those fleeing domestic violence.

Cities like Boston, Worcester, and Springfield bear the brunt of the homelessness crisis in Massachusetts. Concentrated poverty, lack of affordable housing, and limited social services exacerbate the challenges faced by those experiencing homelessness in these urban centers. Escalating housing costs, limited access to affordable healthcare, substance abuse, mental health issues, and unemployment all contribute to the persistent homelessness problem in Massachusetts. Certain populations, such as veterans, youth aging out of foster care, and LGBTQ+

individuals, are disproportionately affected, further highlighting the need for targeted interventions.

While Massachusetts has implemented various initiatives to address homelessness, including emergency shelters, supportive housing programs, rapid rehousing efforts, and collaborations between government agencies, nonprofits, and community organizations, the complexity of the issue necessitates a multifaceted approach. This includes investing in affordable housing development, expanding mental health services, strengthening support systems for at-risk populations, addressing income inequality, and fostering public awareness, empathy, and community engagement. By acknowledging the historical and systemic challenges and working collectively towards solutions, Massachusetts can strive towards a future where everyone has a safe and stable place to call home.

In recent years, innovative approaches have emerged to combat homelessness in Massachusetts. Programs such as Housing First, which prioritize providing stable housing before addressing other needs, have shown promising results in reducing chronic homelessness and improving overall well-being. Advocacy has played a crucial role in addressing homelessness, with activists and organizations advocating for policy changes, increased funding for affordable housing, and improved access to mental health and substance abuse services. Grassroots efforts have brought attention to the needs of those experiencing homelessness and pushed for systemic reforms. However, there is still much work to be done to achieve long-term solutions and create a society where homelessness is seen as a collective responsibility. By acknowledging the multifaceted factors contributing to homelessness and working together, Massachusetts can strive towards a future where everyone has a safe and stable place to call home.

[2] The Historical Context of Homelessness in Massachusetts

Massachusetts has a long and complex history of grappling with the issue of homelessness. The roots of this problem can be traced back to various historical events and societal factors that have shaped the state's landscape.

One significant period that saw a surge in homelessness was the Great Depression of the 1930s. The economic downturn led to widespread poverty, joblessness, and housing insecurity, pushing many individuals and families into homelessness. The lack of a social safety net during this time further exacerbated the crisis.

Another pivotal moment in the history of homelessness in Massachusetts was the deinstitutionalization movement of the 1970s. As mental health facilities closed down across the state, individuals with mental health issues were released into the community without adequate support systems in place. This resulted in a sharp increase in the number of people experiencing homelessness, as many struggled to find stable housing and access the necessary services to address their mental health needs.

In subsequent decades, the state witnessed waves of homelessness driven by economic fluctuations and widening social inequalities. Housing affordability became a pressing concern as rising housing costs outpaced income growth for many individuals and families. This disparity created a situation where individuals were increasingly at risk of losing their homes and falling into homelessness.

Systemic challenges, such as limited access to affordable healthcare, substance abuse issues, and a lack of comprehensive support services, further compounded the homelessness crisis in Massachusetts.

Vulnerable populations, including veterans, youth aging out of foster care, and those facing discrimination, were disproportionately affected by these challenges, leading to higher rates of homelessness within these groups.

Over the years, the state has made efforts to address homelessness through the implementation of various initiatives and programs. Emergency shelters, supportive housing projects, and collaborations between government agencies and nonprofits have aimed to provide temporary relief and long-term solutions for those experiencing homelessness. However, despite these efforts, the issue persists, highlighting the need for a comprehensive and sustained approach.

Understanding the historical context of homelessness in Massachusetts is crucial for developing effective strategies to address the issue. By recognizing the economic fluctuations, social inequalities, and systemic challenges that have contributed to the problem, policymakers, community organizations, and individuals can work together to find lasting solutions and create a society where everyone has access to safe and stable housing.

[3] Current State of Homelessness in Massachusetts

Despite ongoing efforts, the state of Massachusetts still faces a significant homelessness problem. Recent data reveals that on any given night, more than 20,000 individuals find themselves without a home. This staggering number underscores the urgent need for comprehensive and sustainable solutions to address the issue.

The homeless population in Massachusetts encompasses various groups, including families, veterans, individuals with mental health issues, and survivors of domestic violence. The challenges faced by each group are unique and require tailored approaches to effectively address their specific needs.

Homeless families represent a significant portion of the homeless population in Massachusetts. These families often struggle to find stable housing due to the scarcity of affordable options. The lack of affordable housing and the high cost of living place immense pressure on families, leading to housing instability and the risk of homelessness for parents and children alike. The negative impacts of homelessness on children's well-being and educational outcomes are particularly concerning, highlighting the urgent need for targeted interventions and support services.

Veterans experiencing homelessness is another critical issue in Massachusetts. Despite dedicated efforts to address veteran homelessness, many former service members still struggle to access stable housing and necessary support services. The complex challenges faced by veterans, including physical and mental health issues, substance abuse, and limited job opportunities, necessitate comprehensive programs that address these underlying factors.

Individuals with mental health issues are disproportionately affected by homelessness in Massachusetts. The closure of mental health institutions without adequate community-based support systems has resulted in many individuals with mental health challenges lacking the necessary resources and stability to maintain housing. The integration of mental health services with housing initiatives is crucial in effectively addressing homelessness within this population.

Survivors of domestic violence often face homelessness as they flee abusive situations. The lack of affordable housing options, combined with the need for safety and confidentiality, poses significant barriers for individuals seeking to escape domestic violence. Ensuring access to safe and affordable housing, along with specialized support services, is essential in providing survivors with the stability and security they need to rebuild their lives.

Addressing the current state of homelessness in Massachusetts requires a multifaceted approach. Efforts must focus on increasing the availability of affordable housing, expanding supportive housing programs, and improving access to vital support services, including mental health care, substance abuse treatment, and employment assistance.

Collaboration between government agencies, nonprofit organizations, community groups, and individuals is vital in combating homelessness effectively. By working together, stakeholders can pool their resources, expertise, and knowledge to develop innovative strategies and programs that address the root causes of homelessness and provide holistic support to those in need.

While the current homelessness situation in Massachusetts is challenging, it is important to remain hopeful. By recognizing the scale of the problem, implementing evidence-based solutions, and fostering a collective commitment to ending homelessness, Massachusetts can make significant progress towards ensuring that every individual and family has access to safe and stable housing, thereby transforming lives and strengthening communities.

[4] Urban Centers and Homelessness Hotspots

Cities such as Boston, Worcester, and Springfield in Massachusetts bear the brunt of the homelessness crisis within the state. These urban centers face unique challenges and complexities that contribute to the high concentration of homelessness.

One of the key factors amplifying the homelessness crisis in these cities is concentrated poverty. Disadvantaged neighborhoods with limited economic opportunities often experience higher rates of homelessness. Persistent poverty traps individuals and families in a cycle of housing instability, making it difficult to break free from the cycle of homelessness without appropriate support and resources.

A significant contributing factor to homelessness in urban centers is the lack of affordable housing. Massachusetts, particularly in densely populated areas like Boston, faces a shortage of affordable housing options relative to the demand. Rapidly rising housing costs and stagnant wages make it increasingly difficult for low-income individuals and families to secure and maintain housing. This shortage puts vulnerable populations at a heightened risk of homelessness as they struggle to afford stable accommodation.

Limited access to social services further exacerbates the challenges faced by those experiencing homelessness in urban centers. Insufficient funding and resources for outreach programs, mental health services, substance abuse treatment, and employment assistance hinder individuals' ability to address the underlying causes of homelessness and regain stability. The strain on social service agencies and long waiting lists for support exacerbate the difficulties faced by homeless individuals, making it harder for them to navigate the complex system and access the necessary resources.

The visibility of homelessness in urban centers also presents unique challenges for both the homeless population and the community at large. Homelessness is often concentrated in public spaces, such as parks, transit stations, and downtown areas, creating visible reminders of the crisis. This visibility can lead to public concerns about safety, hygiene, and property values, further complicating efforts to address the issue and often resulting in policies that criminalize homelessness rather than providing meaningful solutions.

Efforts to address the homelessness crisis in these urban centers require comprehensive strategies that address the specific needs of the population while considering the unique circumstances of each city. This includes initiatives to increase the availability of affordable housing, expand outreach programs, improve access to social services, and provide targeted support for individuals with mental health issues or substance abuse disorders.

Collaboration between city governments, community organizations, businesses, and residents is crucial in finding sustainable solutions. By engaging in partnerships, stakeholders can work together to develop and implement housing policies, innovative service models, and supportive programs that prioritize long-term housing stability and address the underlying factors driving homelessness in these urban centers.

It is essential to recognize that homelessness is not an isolated issue but a reflection of broader social and economic challenges. By addressing concentrated poverty, increasing affordable housing options, and improving access to comprehensive social services, Massachusetts can begin to alleviate the burden of homelessness in its urban centers and work towards creating inclusive and thriving communities for all residents.

[5] Factors Contributing to Homelessness

The persistent homelessness problem in Massachusetts is influenced by a combination of interconnected factors that contribute to the vulnerability of individuals and families. Understanding these factors is crucial in developing effective strategies to address homelessness. Here are some key contributors to the issue:

- Escalating Housing Costs: High housing costs, particularly in urban areas, strain the budgets of low-income individuals and families. Rising rent prices and limited affordable housing options make it increasingly difficult for those with low incomes to secure and maintain stable housing. The widening gap between income levels and housing costs exacerbates the risk of homelessness.

- Limited Access to Affordable Healthcare: Many individuals experiencing homelessness face barriers in accessing affordable healthcare services. Lack of health insurance, limited healthcare facilities in underserved areas, and the high cost of medical treatments can prevent homeless individuals from receiving the necessary care for both physical and mental health issues. This can contribute to a cycle of homelessness as untreated health conditions can make it challenging to maintain employment or find stable housing.

- Substance Abuse and Addiction: Substance abuse and addiction are prevalent among the homeless population in Massachusetts. Individuals struggling with substance abuse face increased vulnerability to homelessness due to the strain it places on relationships, employment, and personal finances. Substance abuse often exacerbates existing mental health issues and hampers individuals' ability to maintain stable housing.

- Mental Health Issues: A significant proportion of individuals experiencing homelessness in Massachusetts also grapple with mental health challenges. The closure of mental health institutions, insufficient community-based mental health services, and stigma surrounding mental illness contribute to the risk of homelessness for those with untreated or under-treated mental health conditions.

- Unemployment and Underemployment: Limited job opportunities and low wages are contributing factors to homelessness. Unemployment or underemployment, combined with high living costs, can make it impossible for individuals and families to afford housing. Lack of stable income and financial instability can lead to eviction, housing loss, and eventually homelessness.

Addressing these contributing factors requires a comprehensive approach. Strategies may include:

- Increasing the availability of affordable housing through policies such as rent control, affordable housing subsidies, and supportive housing initiatives.

- Improving access to affordable healthcare services by expanding Medicaid coverage, increasing the number of healthcare facilities in underserved areas, and integrating mental health services into primary care settings.

- Enhancing substance abuse treatment and recovery programs, including providing comprehensive support services and increasing funding for substance abuse treatment facilities.

- Expanding mental health services, including outreach programs, counseling, and access to psychiatric care, to ensure individuals receive appropriate care and support.

- Promoting job training and workforce development programs to improve employment opportunities for vulnerable populations, along with advocating for fair wages and worker protections.

By addressing these contributing factors comprehensively, Massachusetts can work towards preventing homelessness and providing the necessary support for individuals and families to regain and maintain stable housing and overall well-being.

[6] Homelessness Among Special Populations

Homelessness in Massachusetts affects certain populations disproportionately, highlighting the unique challenges faced by these vulnerable groups. Understanding these specific circumstances is essential in developing targeted interventions and support systems. Here are some populations that are particularly impacted by homelessness:

- Veterans Returning from Service: Veterans experiencing homelessness is a significant issue in Massachusetts. The transition from military service to civilian life can be challenging, particularly for veterans grappling with physical and mental health issues, substance abuse, and difficulties in finding employment. Inadequate support systems and limited access to veteran-specific services contribute to their higher risk of homelessness.

- Youth Aging Out of Foster Care: Youth aging out of the foster care system are at a heightened risk of homelessness. As they reach adulthood, they often lack stable housing options, financial resources, and a support network. The abrupt transition from foster care to independent living can leave them vulnerable to homelessness and make it challenging to navigate the complexities of securing housing, employment, and education.

- LGBTQ+ Individuals: LGBTQ+ individuals face unique challenges that contribute to their increased risk of homelessness. Discrimination, family rejection, and limited social support networks can lead to housing instability. LGBTQ+ youth, in particular, are disproportionately represented among homeless populations due to family conflict or rejection based on their sexual orientation or gender identity. Access to affirming and inclusive support services is crucial in addressing the specific needs of LGBTQ+ individuals experiencing homelessness.

- Individuals Experiencing Domestic Violence: Survivors of domestic violence often face homelessness as they flee abusive situations. The lack of affordable housing, coupled with the need for safety and confidentiality, poses significant barriers for individuals seeking to escape domestic violence. Ensuring access to safe and affordable housing, along with specialized support services, is essential in providing survivors with the stability and security they need to rebuild their lives.

Efforts to address homelessness among these special populations require tailored approaches. Some strategies include:

- Veteran-Specific Services: Implementing targeted programs that address the unique needs of veterans, including access to healthcare, mental health support, employment assistance, and transitional housing programs specifically designed for veterans.

- Foster Care Transition Support: Providing comprehensive support systems for youth aging out of foster care, including assistance with housing, education, job training, and life skills development to facilitate a successful transition into independent adulthood.

- LGBTQ+ Supportive Services: Ensuring LGBTQ+-affirming services and housing options, as well as training for service providers to create inclusive and safe environments. Advocating for legal protections against discrimination based on sexual orientation and gender identity.

- Domestic Violence Prevention and Support: Strengthening initiatives that provide safe and supportive housing options for survivors of domestic violence, along with access to counseling, legal aid, and advocacy services.

By recognizing and addressing the specific challenges faced by these populations, Massachusetts can strive towards comprehensive solutions that not only address their immediate housing needs but also provide the necessary support systems to prevent homelessness and promote stability, well-being, and inclusion for all.

[7] Challenges Faced by Homeless Families

Homeless families in Massachusetts confront a distinct set of challenges as they strive to provide safe and stable environments for their children. The combination of limited affordable housing options and inadequate support services perpetuates a cycle of instability that significantly impacts the well-being and educational outcomes of children. Recognizing these challenges is crucial in developing effective interventions to break the cycle of homelessness for families.

- Lack of Affordable Housing: One of the primary obstacles faced by homeless families is the scarcity of affordable housing options. Rising housing costs and a shortage of affordable units make it exceedingly difficult for families with limited incomes to secure suitable and stable housing. This lack of affordable housing perpetuates their homelessness and forces them into temporary or inadequate living situations.

- Instability and Disruption: Homelessness disrupts the stability of family life, causing emotional distress and uncertainty for both parents and children. Frequent moves, cramped living conditions, and the lack of a stable home environment can have detrimental effects on the physical and mental well-being of family members. The constant upheaval makes it challenging for children to establish routines, form lasting friendships, and concentrate on their education.

- Educational Disruption: Homelessness often leads to educational disruptions for children. Frequent moves may result in changes in schools, leading to gaps in learning, loss of educational progress, and difficulty adjusting to new academic environments. Limited access to necessary educational resources, such as books, computers, and quiet study spaces, can hinder a child's academic development and hinder their ability to reach their full potential.

- Emotional and Psychological Impact: Homelessness takes a toll on the emotional and psychological well-being of both parents and children. Parents may experience heightened stress, anxiety, and feelings of inadequacy as they struggle to provide for their families. Children may face increased social and emotional challenges, including low self-esteem, depression, and anxiety. The constant instability and the stigma associated with homelessness can have long-lasting effects on their mental health.

- Insufficient Support Services: Homeless families often encounter barriers in accessing necessary support services. Limited availability of emergency shelters, transitional housing, and affordable childcare further compounds the challenges they face. Insufficient resources for counseling, case management, and assistance with finding employment and securing permanent housing make it difficult for families to break free from the cycle of homelessness.

Addressing the challenges faced by homeless families requires a comprehensive approach:

- Increasing Affordable Housing: Expanding the availability of affordable housing options through increased subsidies, rent control policies, and the construction of affordable housing units to ensure that families have access to safe and stable homes.

- Wraparound Support Services: Enhancing support services for homeless families, including access to childcare, mental health counseling, educational support, job training, and financial literacy programs. These services can help parents regain stability and provide a nurturing environment for their children.

- Collaboration and Partnerships: Fostering collaboration between government agencies, non-profit organizations, and community stakeholders to coordinate efforts and resources. Building partnerships with schools, healthcare providers, and social service agencies can ensure a holistic approach to support homeless families and their children.

- Prevention Strategies: Implementing prevention strategies that address the root causes of family homelessness, such as poverty, affordable housing shortages, and access to healthcare. This includes strengthening safety nets, providing financial assistance, and offering early intervention services to at-risk families before they experience homelessness.

By addressing the unique challenges faced by homeless families, Massachusetts can work towards breaking the cycle of homelessness and ensuring that every child has a stable and nurturing environment in which to grow, thrive, and succeed academically and emotionally.

[8] Initiatives and Programs Addressing Homelessness

Massachusetts has implemented a range of initiatives to address the pressing issue of homelessness. These programs and collaborations, involving government agencies, nonprofits, and community organizations, strive to provide both temporary relief and long-term solutions for individuals and families experiencing homelessness. Here are some key initiatives in the state:

- Emergency Shelters: Emergency shelters play a vital role in providing immediate assistance and a safe place to stay for individuals and families facing homelessness. Massachusetts has established a network of emergency shelters that offer temporary accommodations, meals, and supportive services to those in need. These shelters serve as a critical first step in connecting individuals with essential resources and facilitating their transition to more permanent housing solutions.

- Supportive Housing Programs: Supportive housing programs combine affordable housing with supportive services tailored to meet the specific needs of individuals experiencing homelessness. These programs provide stable, permanent housing along with access to case management, mental health services, substance abuse treatment, and job training. By addressing the underlying causes of homelessness, supportive housing programs help individuals regain stability and achieve long-term housing security.

- Rapid Rehousing Efforts: Rapid rehousing programs aim to quickly move individuals and families out of homelessness and into permanent housing. These initiatives provide short-term rental assistance, case management, and financial counseling to help individuals secure housing in the private rental market. By addressing immediate housing needs and providing ongoing support, rapid rehousing efforts prevent prolonged stays in shelters and help individuals maintain housing stability.

-       Collaborations and Partnerships: Collaboration between government agencies, nonprofits, and community organizations is a fundamental aspect of addressing homelessness in Massachusetts. These partnerships facilitate the coordination of resources, knowledge, and expertise, ensuring a comprehensive and unified approach to tackling the issue. Collaborative efforts foster the development of innovative strategies, streamline service delivery, and maximize the impact of available resources.

- Prevention Programs: Recognizing the importance of preventing homelessness, Massachusetts has implemented prevention programs aimed at intervening before individuals and families become homeless. These initiatives include financial assistance, eviction prevention services, and targeted support for at-risk populations. By addressing the root causes of homelessness, prevention programs aim to keep individuals and families housed and mitigate the need for emergency interventions.

- Housing First Approach: Massachusetts has embraced the Housing First approach, which prioritizes providing immediate access to permanent housing for individuals experiencing homelessness, regardless of their readiness for other services. This approach recognizes that stable housing is a fundamental foundation for addressing other needs, such as mental health, substance abuse, and employment. Housing First initiatives focus on rapidly moving individuals into housing and then providing the necessary support services to help them maintain their housing stability.

These initiatives collectively strive to not only provide immediate relief to those experiencing homelessness but also address the underlying factors contributing to homelessness and work towards sustainable, long-term solutions. By combining emergency shelters, supportive housing programs, rapid rehousing efforts, and collaborations between various stakeholders, Massachusetts aims to reduce homelessness and create a more inclusive and supportive society for all residents.

[9] Innovative Approaches and Success Stories

In recent years, Massachusetts has witnessed the emergence of innovative approaches to combat homelessness. These new programs and strategies reflect a shift towards holistic and person-centered approaches, focusing on providing stable housing as the foundation for addressing other needs. One notable example is the Housing First model, which has shown promising results in reducing chronic homelessness and improving overall well-being. Here are some key innovative approaches in Massachusetts:

- Housing First: The Housing First approach prioritizes providing individuals experiencing homelessness with immediate access to stable and permanent housing, without requiring them to meet certain criteria or conditions. This model recognizes that addressing housing instability is crucial for addressing other needs, such as mental health, substance abuse, and employment. By offering housing as the first step, individuals can find stability and security, which can then facilitate their engagement in supportive services tailored to their unique needs.

- Supportive Housing: Supportive housing programs combine affordable housing with wraparound support services tailored to the needs of individuals experiencing homelessness. These programs recognize that housing stability is intertwined with access to comprehensive support systems. Supportive housing initiatives provide on-site case management, mental health services, substance abuse treatment, job training, and other services to address the underlying factors contributing to homelessness. This integrated approach helps individuals maintain housing stability and improve their overall well-being.

- Housing Navigation Programs: Housing navigation programs focus on assisting individuals and families in navigating the complex process of finding and securing housing. Housing navigators work closely with clients, providing personalized support, advocacy, and assistance in accessing affordable housing options. These programs address the barriers faced by individuals experiencing homelessness, such as lack of knowledge about available resources, difficulties in understanding housing applications, and limited access to transportation.

- Data-Driven Solutions: Massachusetts has embraced data-driven solutions to tackle homelessness effectively. By analyzing data on homelessness patterns, service utilization, and outcomes, policymakers and service providers can identify gaps, measure progress, and allocate resources more efficiently. This approach helps in tailoring interventions, targeting resources where they are most needed, and evaluating the effectiveness of programs in reducing homelessness.

- Cross-Sector Collaborations: Collaboration between government agencies, nonprofits, healthcare providers, and community organizations is essential in implementing innovative approaches to homelessness. Cross-sector collaborations foster the sharing of expertise, resources, and best practices. By combining the strengths of various stakeholders, these collaborations enhance the effectiveness of interventions, improve service coordination, and create a comprehensive safety net for individuals and families experiencing homelessness.

These innovative approaches in Massachusetts reflect a growing recognition that addressing homelessness requires more than just providing emergency shelters. By prioritizing stable housing and incorporating supportive services, Massachusetts aims to break the cycle of homelessness and improve the well-being and quality of life for individuals and families. Continued exploration of innovative strategies, coupled with ongoing evaluation and refinement, will contribute to the long-term success in combating homelessness in the state.

[10] Advocacy and Policy Changes

Advocacy has proven to be a vital force in addressing homelessness in Massachusetts. Activists, organizations, and grassroots efforts have played a crucial role in advocating for policy changes, increased funding for affordable housing, and improved access to vital services. Their collective efforts have brought attention to the needs of individuals experiencing homelessness and pushed for systemic reforms. Here are key ways in which advocacy has made a difference:

- Policy Reform: Advocacy groups have been instrumental in advocating for policy changes to address homelessness. They have worked tirelessly to influence legislation, regulations, and local ordinances to prioritize affordable housing, homelessness prevention, and supportive services. By engaging with policymakers and stakeholders, advocacy efforts have led to the implementation of more progressive and inclusive policies that aim to address the root causes of homelessness.

- Increased Funding: Advocacy campaigns have played a significant role in securing increased funding for affordable housing programs, homelessness prevention initiatives, and support services. By raising awareness about the impact of homelessness and the need for adequate resources, advocates have successfully mobilized public support and secured government funding to expand programs that provide housing options and wraparound support.

- Awareness and Education: Advocacy efforts have played a crucial role in raising awareness about homelessness and dispelling misconceptions. By organizing events, campaigns, and educational initiatives, advocates have shed light on the complexities of homelessness and highlighted the systemic factors that contribute to it. They have worked to foster empathy, reduce stigma, and promote understanding, fostering a more compassionate and supportive community.

- Coalition Building: Advocacy organizations have fostered coalitions and partnerships among various stakeholders, including nonprofits, service providers, community members, and policymakers. By uniting diverse voices and perspectives, these coalitions amplify the advocacy efforts, increase their collective impact, and ensure that the needs of individuals experiencing homelessness are addressed comprehensively and holistically.

- Grassroots Mobilization: Grassroots efforts have been at the forefront of advocacy for homelessness. Community-based organizations, activists, and individuals directly affected by homelessness have mobilized to bring attention to the issue. Through protests, public demonstrations, storytelling, and engagement with local media, grassroots advocates have put pressure on decision-makers to prioritize homelessness as a pressing social issue and to take meaningful action.

- Systemic Reforms: Advocacy has been pivotal in driving systemic reforms to address the underlying causes of homelessness. By advocating for affordable housing policies, improvements in access to mental health and substance abuse services, and equitable social policies, advocates work towards creating a society that prevents homelessness and provides a safety net for those who experience it.

The power of advocacy lies in its ability to elevate the voices of individuals experiencing homelessness, create a sense of urgency, and drive policy changes and resource allocation. By working collectively, advocates have made significant strides in addressing homelessness in Massachusetts and continue to push for sustainable solutions and social justice. Their efforts serve as a reminder that meaningful change is possible when communities unite to fight for a more equitable and compassionate society.

[11] Moving Forward: Potential Solutions and the Role of Society

Addressing homelessness in Massachusetts requires a multifaceted approach that encompasses various strategies and interventions. To effectively tackle the issue and work towards sustainable solutions, the following elements should be prioritized:

- Affordable Housing Development: Investing in the development of affordable housing is crucial in providing stable and accessible housing options for individuals and families experiencing homelessness. This involves increasing the availability of affordable housing units, implementing rent control policies, and expanding housing subsidies to ensure that housing is affordable for all income levels.

- Expanded Mental Health Services: Addressing mental health challenges is essential in preventing and addressing homelessness. Investing in accessible and comprehensive mental health services, including counseling, therapy, and psychiatric care, helps individuals experiencing homelessness receive the necessary support to address mental health issues and regain stability.

- Strengthened Support Systems for At-Risk Populations: Vulnerable populations, such as veterans, youth aging out of foster care, and individuals experiencing domestic violence, require targeted support systems to prevent homelessness. This involves developing specialized programs that provide housing assistance, case management, job training, and educational support tailored to the unique needs of these populations.

- Addressing Income Inequality: Income inequality is a significant driver of homelessness. Addressing this issue requires efforts to increase wages, improve job opportunities, and implement policies that promote economic equity. This includes advocating for a livable minimum wage, expanding job training programs, and supporting small businesses to stimulate local economies.

- Prevention and Early Intervention: Emphasizing prevention and early intervention strategies is crucial in minimizing the risk of homelessness. This involves providing financial assistance to individuals and families facing eviction, offering support services to those at risk of homelessness, and implementing effective outreach programs to identify and assist individuals before they become homeless.

- Public Awareness and Empathy: Increasing public awareness and fostering empathy are essential components of addressing homelessness. By educating the public about the complex factors contributing to homelessness and dispelling stereotypes and stigmas, communities can cultivate a more compassionate understanding of the issue. Public awareness campaigns, community forums, and educational initiatives can promote empathy, foster community engagement, and encourage individuals to take action.

- Community Engagement and Collaboration: Engaging community members, organizations, and stakeholders in addressing homelessness is crucial for creating sustainable and impactful solutions. Building partnerships between government agencies, nonprofits, faith-based organizations, businesses, and community groups can leverage resources, knowledge, and expertise to develop comprehensive approaches that address the diverse needs of individuals experiencing homelessness.

By combining efforts to invest in affordable housing, expand mental health services, strengthen support systems, address income inequality, promote public awareness and empathy, and foster community engagement, Massachusetts can work towards reducing homelessness and creating a society where housing stability is a collective responsibility. It is through this multifaceted approach that lasting change can be achieved, ensuring that every individual has access to safe, affordable housing and the support they need to thrive.

[12] Towards a Future of Housing Stability

The homelessness situation in Massachusetts is undoubtedly a complex issue shaped by historical and systemic challenges. While progress has been made through various initiatives, advocacy efforts, and innovative approaches, it is essential to recognize that there is still much work to be done. By acknowledging the multifaceted factors contributing to homelessness and working collectively to address them, Massachusetts can strive towards a future where everyone has a safe and stable place to call home. Here are key considerations moving forward:

- Continued Collaboration: Collaboration between government entities, nonprofits, community organizations, and individuals with lived experiences is vital. By working together, sharing knowledge and resources, and fostering open dialogue, stakeholders can develop comprehensive and inclusive solutions that address the diverse needs of those experiencing homelessness.

- Long-Term Housing Solutions: While emergency shelters and temporary interventions are crucial, investing in long-term housing solutions is paramount. This includes increasing the availability of affordable housing units, exploring alternative housing models, and prioritizing supportive housing programs that combine housing with essential services tailored to individuals' unique needs.

-    Comprehensive Support Services: Accessible and comprehensive support services are crucial in addressing the underlying causes of homelessness. This includes expanding mental health services, substance abuse treatment programs, employment assistance, and educational support. By providing a holistic approach, individuals experiencing homelessness can rebuild their lives and achieve long-term stability.

- Prevention and Early Intervention: Preventing homelessness before it occurs is a cost-effective and compassionate approach. This involves implementing robust eviction prevention programs, financial assistance for at-risk individuals and families, and early intervention initiatives that address the root causes of homelessness before they escalate.

- Addressing Structural Inequalities: Homelessness is closely intertwined with structural inequalities, such as income disparities, discrimination, and systemic barriers. By actively addressing these issues, Massachusetts can work towards creating a more equitable society where housing stability is a reality for all residents.

- Advocacy and Policy Reform: Advocacy efforts must continue to push for policy changes and increased funding for homelessness prevention and affordable housing initiatives. By amplifying the voices of those affected by homelessness, advocating for systemic reforms, and holding policymakers accountable, progress can be made towards lasting change.

- Public Education and Empathy: Building public awareness and empathy is crucial in combating homelessness. By fostering a deeper understanding of the complexities and individual stories behind homelessness, communities can promote empathy, reduce stigma, and encourage engagement in finding solutions.

- The path towards resolving homelessness in Massachusetts requires a collective commitment and sustained effort. By acknowledging the historical and systemic challenges, investing in affordable housing, expanding support services, addressing inequalities, advocating for policy reforms, and fostering empathy, the state can move closer to a future where every individual has a safe and stable place to call home.

[13] Conclusion

The issue of homelessness in Massachusetts is a complex and persistent challenge that requires a comprehensive and compassionate response. While progress has been made through initiatives, advocacy, and innovative approaches, there is still much work to be done to address the root causes and provide sustainable solutions. By investing in affordable housing development, expanding access to mental health services, strengthening support systems for at-risk populations, addressing income inequality, and fostering public awareness and empathy,

Massachusetts can strive towards a future where homelessness is no longer a prevalent issue.

It is crucial to recognize the multifaceted nature of homelessness and the diverse needs of those affected by it. By implementing long-term housing solutions, comprehensive support services, prevention and early intervention strategies, and by addressing structural inequalities, Massachusetts can create a more equitable society where housing stability is accessible to all residents.

Additionally, the power of advocacy and community engagement should not be underestimated. Through continued advocacy efforts, policy reform, and grassroots mobilization, we can bring about meaningful change and hold decision-makers accountable. It is through public education, empathy, and collective responsibility that we can foster a society where homelessness is seen as an issue that affects us all, and where every individual has the opportunity for a safe and stable place to call home.

While the journey to address homelessness in Massachusetts may be challenging, it is a journey worth embarking on. By acknowledging the historical and systemic challenges, implementing evidence-based solutions, and working together as a community, we can create lasting change and ensure a future where homelessness becomes a rarity rather than a prevalent reality. Let us strive towards a Massachusetts where everyone has the opportunity to thrive and where no one is left without a place to call home.

Unveiling the Invisible

Exploring Homelessness in Massachusetts

By

Dr. David K. Ewen, Minister

www.ingramcontent.com/pod-product-compliance
Lightning Source LLC
Chambersburg PA
CBHW051757250726
48659CB00001B/460